The
World's
Greatest
Golf
Jokes

Stan McDougal

The World's Greatest Golf Jokes

Drawings by Wallop Manyum

CITADEL PRESS   SECAUCUS, N.J.

Second paperbound printing

Copyright © 1980 by Citadel Press
All rights reserved
Published by Citadel Press
A division of Lyle Stuart Inc.
120 Enterprise Ave., Secaucus, N.J. 07094
In Canada: General Publishing Co. Limited
Don Mills, Ontario
Manufactured in the United States of America

Library of Congress Cataloging in Publication Data
Diamant, Lincoln.
    The world's greatest golf jokes.
    1.   Golf—Anecdotes, facetiae, satire, etc.
I.   Title.
GV967.D53   796.352'0207   80-19937

"Do you miss playing golf?"
"Nobody's perfect."

*This book is for Linc Diamant,
without whose patience and unfailing good humor
it would never have been possible.*

Contents

Introduction

Human perversity often leads us to mock our most sacred institutions.

Golf is no exception.

Bennett Cerf—quite a storyteller himself—once exegesized the situation on "What's My Line?":

> *The game of golf was launched at 11:10 A.M.,*
> *the first lie about a scorecard at 11:22, and the*
> *first golf joke at noon.*

That first joke was naturally about a Scot named Fergus, and you'll find it neatly printed at the top of page 158.

Not unlike eating potato chips, that joke led to another ... and another ... and finally, to this volume. Because, compared to compulsively telling funny stories to your friends, nothing beats sitting down and putting them all together in a book.

So this collection slowly came into being, thanks to conscientious listening all over the globe—while playing golf courses, drinking in clubhouse bars, or sitting around board room conferences . . . eavesdropping everywhere members of the golf tribe gather to exchange their hopes and fears. Now you hold the result in your hands—an authoritative compendium of what are, beyond any reasonable doubt, several hundred of the world's greatest golf jokes and stories.

We hope you'll discover here enough retellable japery to coax a grin from the most case-hardened devotee of the well-rolled green. Your own golfing experience may even evoke a titter or two. Chinese and Russians are excused from smiling; they have other problems and no golf courses.

It's a volume chock-a-block with relatively innocent merriment—whether or not you are married to the world's most unfunny sport, or merely like to giggle at those who are. Contemporary unisex trends have suggested minimal attempts to create side-splitting analogous facetiae out of outstanding male or female sex characteristics.

And since authors should try to be humble (and always work towards the Second Edition), purposely omitted on the following pages is my own favorite golf joke (told to me by Mr. J). But amidst all the other ribaldry, you'll scarcely miss it.

So, "Fore!"

—STAN McDOUGAL

Before the Game

"Is this Harry's secretary? I forgot to ask him which course we're playing on this afternoon."

"Sorry, Mr. Nash is out of the office all day on business."

"You're *supposed* to say that, but which course will we be on?"

"Sorry, Mr. Nash is out on a business call."

"O.K., O.K. Just tell me. Is his call three or 18 miles from the office?"

"What would you say to a round of golf?"
"Generally I don't speak unless spoken to."

"Sometimes research takes you fairly far afield. Margaret Mead lived five years in a place where natives beat the ground with clubs and uttered blood-curdling yells."

"Gosh, Prof, they miss putts in New Guinea, too?"

A Scots Highlander came to attention in the pro shop of the Royal and Ancient Golf Club of St. Andrews. He held out a badly-nicked ball.

"Weel," said the pro, "we can vulcanize it for two shillings, or re-cover it complete for four."

"Tomorra," said the Highlander, "ye shall have tha' answer."

The next day he was back, holding out the ball. "Tha' Regiment," he said, "votes ta' vulcanize."

Sign on locker room mirror: ALSO LOOK BACKING UP—IN CASE YOU PLAY THROUGH.

"Johnny! Remember what happens to little boys who use bad language playing marbles!"

"Yep, teacher. They grow up, and play golf."

"Dad, I've decided. I want to be a golf bum."

"Do you really think I'll let you spend the best years of your life tramping around the golf course?"

"Can you afford a cart?"

Then there was the hooker who asked a secretary if she'd like to join her on a pro-am.

A Scotsman who had been playing the links at Pitlochry for 25 years with the same ball, decided the time had finally come to buy a new one.

He walked into the Pitlochry pro shop and announced sourly, "Weel, here I am ageen."

"How can you possibly practice golf in the winter time?"

"I swing my umbrella on the way to work, curse everybody in the office, have a double Scotch, and come home."

"Why so late teeing off?"

"It's Sunday. Tossed a coin between church and golf."

"But why *so* late?"

"Had to toss fifteen times."

Then there was the completely unabridged dictionary of golfing terms that was banned from the mails.

"Come over for a couple of beers, Harry?"

"Can't today. McDougal's playing in the Club Tournament."

NEXT WEEK:

"Come over for a few beers, Harry?"

"Can't make it this week, either. McDougal won at the Club. He's playing in the All-Island."

NEXT WEEK:

"How about some beers *today*, Harry?"

"No good. McDougal has moved up to the State Open."

"Say, Harry, your game used to be *basketball*. How come this sudden interest in golf; always watching McDougal?"

"I don't watch McDougal. Whenever he plays, I make out with his wife."

"I've invented a new game resembling golf."

"That's nothing *new*. I've been playing it for years!"

"Swing without striking the ball," counseled the pro at the Royal Quebec Course.

"That," replied the novice, "is exactly what I'm trying to *correct!*"

"Playing golf might improve your health."

"But Doc, I've been golfing for sixteen years!"

"In that case, better quit."

A player at the Troon Golf Club in Ayrshire bought himself a new golf bag at the pro shop.

"Shall I wrap it for you?" asked the pro.

"Nae, laddie. But be kind eno' to put th' string and paper inside."

"Darling, remember the day we were married?"
"Sure do. Sank a 35-foot putt the day before."

"Can ye stamp ma' name on this ball in case I lose it?"
a player asked the pro at Scotland's Nairn Golf Club.
   "To be sure."
   "An' can ye also put an 'M.D.' after it?"
   "Possibly."
   "An' then ha' aboot, 'Hours 9 to 4, except Tuesdays'?"

"Dad, remember the $500 you promised me for my
first hole-in-one?"
   "Yes?"
   "Can I borrow against the interest?"

"My brother-in-law's discovered a new way to take off strokes."

"An eraser?"

It was hard to tell—Will Rogers once suggested—whether the American people became such liars because of income tax or golf.

"Playing today, Harry?"

"Nope. Just joined 'Golfers Anonymous.' "

"Wotthell's *that*?"

"Whenever you feel like a game, someone comes over and drinks with you instead."

"My barber has a special formula that can even grow hair on a golf ball."

"Absolutely marvelous!"

"No way."

"Why not?"

"Slows the hell out of his game."

"Did my sermon bore you, my son?"

"Nooooo, Father. Why do you ask?"

"You appeared to be holding the hymnal in an overlapping grip."

An American stops a passerby on the High Street of Fife: "How do I get to the Royal and Ancient Golf Club of St. Andrews?"

Replies the Scot, "Practice, laddie, practice!"

"Golf, golf! Harry, I'd drop dead if you ever spent a Sunday at home!"

"Trying to bribe me?"

"Father, is it a sin in the eyes of the Lord to play golf on Sunday?"

"The way you play, my son, it's a sin any day."

"Sorry, hon, but I gotta' get up, shower and meet my buddies for a round of golf."

"Darling! It's only five in the morning. And we were married just yesterday afternoon!"

"Sorry, sweets. I guess I forgot to tell you. I'm a real golf freak."

"*A real golf freak!* Well I forgot to tell *you*! I'm a real hooker."

"That's all right. Just shift your left thumb down and over a bit. You'll be O.K."

"What's the quickest way to beat my brother-in-law at golf?"

"Give him a book on how to play."

In the immoral words of Lisle Trauts:

"Give me my golf clubs, the fresh air and a beautiful partner . . . and you can keep my golf clubs and the fresh air."

"What will go best with my pink and purple golf socks?"

"Hip boots."

"Just got a brand new set of clubs for my wife."

"Excellent trade!"

"How can I improve on 36 holes of golf a week, roughly speaking?"

"Stop cursing."

Then there was the wealthy Saudi Arabian who ordered a matched set of fourteen clubs—each with Olympic-sized pool.

"Would you like to learn to play golf, madam?" inquired the pro.

"No, thank you. But ask my friend there. I *already* learned yesterday."

Halfway across the Atlantic on an Aer Lingus excursion to the Masters in Atlanta, two Irish pros were interrupted by the pilot's intercom: "We've gone and lost an ingine. However, we can sthill fly on the ither three."

A half hour later came a second report: "We've lost anither ingine, but iverything will still be all right."

Half an hour later, the *third* engine quit. With that announcement, one pro turned to his partner: "Begorrah! If we go and lose that fourth ingine, we'll not only miss the tee-off; we'll be up here all night!"

"Let's stop at the clubhouse and pick up a fifth for golf."

"You mean a fourth."

"No, I'm thirsty."

"Understand your new boy friend is actually a poor golfer."

"That sonofagun told me he was a rich banker."

"Your damn game's so important, you haven't even noticed this lovely Sunday breakfast you're eating."

"Sure I have, dear. Pass the putter."

Teeing Off

The pickup threesome at the municipal course—a gentleman with a thick beard, a clean-shaven middle-aged man with rimless glasses, and a pert young redhead—exchanged tee-off introductions:

"My name is Ben Ezra. But I'm not the Rabbi."

"My name is Francis Xavier. But I'm not a Saint."

"My n-n-n-name is M-M-M-Mary, and I'm not a v-v-v-v-v-very good player."

"I guess I'm your partner today—Philip Alcott Starnes II."

"Sorry. I only go around with winners."

"I sent my golf club manufacturer a photo of me teeing off, for his advertising."

"Any reply?"

"What's an 'injunction'?"

"Funny golf socks you're wearing, one yellow and the other green."

"What's funny? Got another pair just like 'em at home."

"You don't mind carrying all our bags, do you?" a threesome asked a caddy at Peekskill, N.Y.'s Mohansic Golf Course.

"No problem," replied the youngster, "just so long as you sling a couple of concrete blocks around my neck."

"What for!"

"Just to keep me from breaking into a run."

"Caddymaster, that boy isn't even eight years old."
"Better that way, sir. He probably can't count past ten."

An obese Maori chief took up the game at New Zealand's Otago Golf Club at Balmacewen.

But when he put the ball where he could see it, he couldn't hit it. And when he put the ball where he could hit it, he couldn't see it.

"How come your husband bought you that fancy new golf bag?"
"Caught him fooling with the maid."
"How dreadful! Did you fire her?"
"No. I need some new clubs, too."

"First tee the ball."
"I tee it. What cwub do I use?"

"You really shouldn't be playing off the ladies' tee."
"I'm not. I've duffed three times."

"That's your twelfth whiff and now you're *really* not addressing the ball properly."
"Good manners can be carried too far."

"Why are you using *two* caddies today?"
"Wife feels I don't spend enough time with my kids."

"I usually shoot in the low 90's."
"Kinda' hot to play golf."

While waiting to tee off at the annual company outing, the boss was telling golf joke after golf joke. Everyone in the firm was laughing uproariously—except one employee who stood around with a very long face.

"Don't you think he's funny?" asked one of his co-workers.

"No," was the reply, "and I'm quitting Friday anyway."

"Sorry, sir," the caddymaster told a player waiting to tee off at Palm Beach's Seminole Country Club, "You can't play today. None of the caddies came in."

"So give me a Buick?"

"No one told me this would be a *mixed* foursome."

"That's just my brother-in-law. He's got problems."

"Can't get the four of you off today, sir. Really crowded."

"And what if Crenshaw, Nicklaus, Irwin and Green showed up?"

"Oh! We'd have to give *them* a round."

"Well, they're playing the Masters. We'll just take their spot."

"Usual handicap today?"
"Yep. The wife and kids."

"Who do you like caddying for, left- or right-handed golfers?"
"Don't make no difference, sir. Just so they're not lefties who keep their money in their right hand."

"I shoot in the low 70's."
"Honestly?"
"What's that got to do with it?"

"Harry, I've swung at the ball fourteen times and haven't hit it yet."

"Keep trying, dear. It's beginning to look a bit worried."

Sign at Royal Aberdeen Golf Club: *Please! Don't Pick Up Lost Balls . . . Until They've Stopped Rolling.*

One Saturday at the Rye, N.Y., municipal course, a little man kept inching his way toward the head of the long line of golfers waiting to tee off. Each time, he was tossed back unceremoniously to where he had started.

"Once more," he finally warned the line, "And I won't open the course!"

"Caddy, tell me how to address the ball."

"Just so they can get it back to you once you lose it, sir."

"Caddy, are you good at finding lost balls?"

"Best around, sir."

"Then find one, and we'll get started."

"Got fired from your caddy job?"

"Yep. Couldn't learn not to laugh out loud."

"No matter what I do, I always seem to top the ball."

"Why not try teeing it upside down."

"I think that golfer's nattily attired."
"In *men's* clothes?"

"Do you have a handicap?"
"Only that I try not to cheat."

Then there was the old duffer who had been around so long his handicap was in Roman numerals.

"Caddy, how much are 4 and 5 and 3?"
"Nine."
"You'll be just fine."

Mulligan

From the 1st tee at Springfield, New Jersey's Baltusrol Country Club, a player blasted a mighty drive that was picked up by a following gale, floated 465 yards down the fairway, onto the green, past the pin and into the cup!

"Not bad!" his partner commented, "Now I'll take *my* practice shot, and we can get started."

1st HOLE

On the 1st tee at the Royal Cape Town Golf Club, a novice drove off—directly into a tree. The ball, striking at just the right angle, came screaming back past the caddy. The golfer dropped his club, raising his hands just in time to catch the ball and keep himself from being struck in the head.

Regaining his composure, he turned to the caddy. "What should I do now?" he asked.

"Why not try the same shot again, sir? But this time, keep your hands in your pockets."

An Australian novice aced the 1st hole at Victoria's Royal Melbourne . . . then reached for another ball, saying, "I think I've got the hang of this bloody game!"

A drunk playing golf with a nun.

At the 1st tee, he swings wildly. "Dammit," he says, "I missed!"

The nun frowns.

The drunk swings a second time . . . and misses again. "Dammit! I missed."

The nun looks stern . . . but says nothing.

One more swing—one more miss—one more, "Dammit! I missed."

This time the nun coughs, and says, "Sir, should you continue to use foul language, the heavens may open up . . . the Good Lord may strike you down with a thunderbolt."

The drunk stands quiet for a moment, then addresses the ball again, swings . . . and misses. "DAMMIT! I missed."

The heavens split asunder. A lightning bolt comes down and kills . . . the nun.

A mighty voice rings through the universe: *"DAMMIT! I MISSED!"*

"Wow, caddy! Look at that ball go! About time, too, after five strokes on the tee."

"That's not the ball, sir. Your wristwatch."

"Caddy, when do I get to use the putter?"
"Please, sir, sometime before dark."

On the first tee at Australia's Indooroopilly Golf Club, a visiting American swung his driver wildly over the ball.

"That's interesting," he apologized, "Your course seems about two inches lower than the one at home."

Zeus invited Hector and Achilles to play golf.

He teed off first along a beautiful fairway lined with olive trees. His drive ricocheted back and forth from tree to tree. The ball finally made the green, rolled—and dropped into the cup.

Achilles roared angrily:

"Πρόσεξε, Δία. Πρόκειται γιά παιγνίδι χρήματος. Θά παίξης τώρα γκόλφ ἤ θά κοροϊδεύης?" *

* "Look, Zeus. This is a money game. You going to play golf, or screw around?"

On Husband-and-Wife Day at La Quinta in Palm Springs, a player drove straight down the 1st fairway. Taking over, his wife sliced the ball 100 yards into the rough. The husband gritted his teeth and made a magnificent recovery right onto the green. The wife blasted her putt past the pin into a deep trap. Delicately, the man lifted the ball back to the green—where it rolled into the cup.

He turned to his wife. "We'll have to do a *bit* better than that from now on, dear. The hole was a bogey five."

"Don't give *me* a hard time," she snapped, "only *two* of those strokes were *mine*."

"Your score on the hole so far?"
"Two."
"Two! I thought I counted *three*!"
"One was only a practice swing."
"Then why'd you curse?"

"Why didn't you see where my ball went, caddy?"
"Sorry, sir. I wasn't expecting it to go anywhere."

"Why're you playing with *two* caddies today?"
"Last time around, I had to get rid of one for laughing."

Two idiots playing golf.

The first shuts his eyes, swings mightily—and drops an unbelievable hole-in-one.

"Bet you can't do *that* again," says the other.

"How much?"

"$100."

"One condition."

"Whazzat?"

"This time I can get to keep my eyes open!"

Jesus tees off on the Heavenly Links—with a terrible slice. The ball disappears deep in the rough. Silence. Suddenly, a rabbit darts out onto the fairway with the ball in its mouth. An eagle swoops down and carries the rabbit over the green. The balls drops from the rabbit's mouth directly into the cup.

St. Peter turns to Jesus and says:

"Very funny. Now play golf!"

A novice at Antigua's Half-Moon Bay Course faded a long drive off the 1st tee that bounced—in quick succession—off a tree, a golf cart, a coral outcrop and a ball washer; and then rolled onto the green within two inches of the cup.

"Goddam!" exclaimed the amateur, "if only I'd hit that mother a bit harder!"

ECUMENICAL JOKE (fill in your blanks):

A truant _____ (priest) (rabbi) was playing an otherwise deserted course on _____ _____ (Good Friday) (Yom Kippur).

From the first tee, he drove the green 415 yards—right into the cup!

He shook an angry fist at heaven. "My very first ace— and now whom can I tell?"

On the 1st tee of Chaska, Minnesota's Hazeltine National Country Club, a complete novice asked his caddy, "How does one play this game?"

"See that little flag, sir? Just hit the ball in that direction."

The novice uncorked an absolutely incredible drive.

At the green, the caddy couldn't believe his eyes—the ball lay only three inches from the cup. He jumped up and down excitedly.

"What do I do here?" asked the player, coming up.

"Get the ball into the cup. sir!"

"NOW he tells me!"

"Now I'm in *real* trouble," exclaimed the novice as he sank a long putt on the 1st at Hot Springs' Homestead Course.

"Why, sir?" asked his caddy.

"I can't remember which club gets it out."

2nd HOLE

A novice on Denmark's Helsingor Golf Club teed up the first ball in his life, shut his eyes, swung—and sank a hole-in-one!

From the 2nd tee, he again drove with a mighty smash that carried right to the green and up to the edge of the unattended flagstick—where the ball teetered—and dropped into the cup!

"Thank God!" he exclaimed, "For a moment there, I thought I'd missed."

"I want to be a golfer in the worst way, caddy."
"Stop now, sir. You're way ahead."

During a strike of caddies on the Cloister Course at Sea Island, Georgia, a twosome on the 2nd watched with amazement as another golfer approached the green with his bag strapped to a huge St. Bernard.

"Now there's a guy who's really clever," commented one player loudly.

"He's not so smart," said the dog, "Still asks me which club to use."

"What sort of ball did you lose?"
"Brand new. Not even properly hit yet."

"You can only count to four?" an American visitor inquired of his caddy on the panoramic course at Pevero in Sardinia.
"Thats'a right, sir."
"Wonderful! By the way, what did you write down for that first hole?"
"Two'a threes."

A golfer yells, "Fore!", takes six, and writes, "5."

On the 2nd green of the Chicago Country Club Course at Wheaton, a meticulous player studied every angle of a three-foot putt, flecked a piece of grass from the lip of the cup, tried the wind with a wet finger, and queried his caddy, "Was the green mowed this morning?"

"Yessir," was the reply.

"Left to right, or right to left?"

"Right to left nap, sir."

The golfer putted—and missed badly. He whirled on the caddy, "What TIME?"

Technological improvement over the caddy: the golf cart. *It can't count or criticize.*

Then there was the spectator who walked out on the 2nd hole of the Second Round at the Masters—because that was where she had come in.

Golf: A game where everyone in front is too slow, and everyone behind is too fast.

After the 1st hole at Edinburgh's Duddingston Golf Course, a Scots player turned to his American guest. "Ha' many strokes d'ye have?"
"Eight."
"I took seven. Ma' hole."
After the 2nd hole, the Scot repeated the question.
"Nossir!" said the American, "*My* turn to ask."

Nothing counts in a golf game like your opponent.

"Your husband seems to be hitting the ball better, with that new stance."

"Old stance. New husband."

"How long have you been playing golf?"

"Three months."

"Pretty good for three months!"

"Been *learning* to play for seven years."

3rd HOLE

A player blasted out of a 3rd hole trap onto the green at Pittsburgh's Oakmont Golf Course. But by the cup he found only an alluring young golfer—his ball was nowhere to be seen. "Did a ball just roll up here?" he inquired.

"Search me," replied the girl.

"Swell. But first let's find my ball."

When you drink don't drive. *Certainly* don't putt.

An American driving between huge sand hills on County Kerry's Ballybunion Course called, "Fore!", swung blindly—and struck a local crossing the 3rd fairway.

"Murtherer!" cried the Irishman, advancing on the golfer.

"But I called, 'Fore!' That's the signal to get out of my way."

"Well, when I call, 'Foive,' that's the signal to bust yer jaw! Foive!"

"Harry, I think my swing's improving!"
"Why's that, dear?"
"I'm missing the ball much closer than I used to."

The caddy watched as the minister drove four balls into the water hazard, broke his clubs, threw his tees into the woods and announced, "I'm giving it up!"

"The game?" asked the caddy.

"No, the ministry."

Two golfers took shelter beneath a giant oak tree near Augusta National's 3rd hole to avoid a sudden thunderstorm.

One pulled out their scorecard. "What did you have on that last hole?"

"Six."

CRASH! CRACK! LIGHTNING!

"Better make that a *seven*."

A hole-in-one on the 1st.

Another ace on the 2nd!

But on the 3rd, the tee shot merely rolled past the cup.

The novice turned to his caddy: "Oh, well. A beginner's still a beginner."

"Watch out for that clump of bushes near the green on this 3rd hole," a woman advised her partner at Detroit's Grosse Point Farms Country Club.

"Why?"

"That's where those awful caddies *always* try to sneak away!"

"Good Lord, Mildred! I think I just sank a hole-in-one."

"Do it again, dear. I wasn't looking."

"Why do ministers play such poor golf?"

"They have no vocabulary for it."

"Forget it, caddy. A guy who can hit a ball like that doesn't deserve to get it back."

"Oh, no, sir. A guy who can hit a ball like that certainly deserves a souvenir."

Show me a sportsman who's a good loser and I'll show you a man playing golf with his boss.

"Where's the best course in Alaska?"

"Juneau."

"If I did, I wouldn't ask."

4th HOLE

An American on the Ostschweizerischer Course was being driven out of his mind by a hiccuping Swiss caddy. Stroke after stroke, he kept hooking his ball off the fairway into the melting snow.

On the 4th, however, he drove a tremendous slice that disappeared in a crevasse.

"Goddam caddy!" he screamed at his partner.

"But he didn't hiccup that time!"

"That time I finally made allowance!"

"What makes you think McGruder used to be in construction?"

"The way he spits on his hands every time he picks up a club."

GOLF: Eighteen irregular intervals of frustration mixed with several columns of poor arithmetic.

As the waters of Calibogue Sound lapped quietly in the background, an older golfer on the Harbor Town Course at Hilton Head reminisced: "I can still remember the first time I saw a miniskirt on these links."

"When was that?"

"Here on the 4th green. Missed my 6-inch putt."

Golf is for backward Americans: they talk nothing but golf in the office and nothing but business on the links.

"Just spent $1,000 on this full set of clubs, caddy."

"It's worth it, sir."

"Why's that?"

"You certainly use them in rotation."

A solitary player, whiffing badly on the 4th tee of Perthshire's Blairgowie Course, watched a poacher crossing the rough carrying a shotgun.

"Hoot, mon!" he called, "Only golfers allow'd on tha' course!"

"If *ye* dinna' tell," came the reply, "*I* dinna' tell."

"That's my new girl friend. This summer she's taken up golf."

"How's her game?"

"She's going around in less and less."

"I can see that; but how's her game?"

"Bet you a dime you can't sink that putt."

"I don't bet that kind of money."

"O.K. Take part of it."

"If we quit right now, we could still make church."

"Not me. I'd have to go back and take care of the wife. She's dying."

"How about that shot, caddy!" a golfer cried exultantly at the hazardous dog-leg on the 4th at Mamaroneck's Winged Foot Golf Club, "Could Nicklaus ever have gotten out of *that*?"

"Nicklaus never would have gotten *in*, sir."

"Like my game, caddy?"

"Not bad, sir. But I still prefer golf."

"Your putting's better than ever. Are those bifocals?"

"Damn right! Now I just knock the *little* ball into the *big* hole."

"The pro on this course makes more money than the President of the United States."

"Why not? He plays a helluva better game."

A golfer turned to his partner on the 4th hole at the Doral Country Club. "Oh, my God," he recalled, "I think we forgot to lock the safe!"

"Don't worry, Harry. We're both *here* in Miami."

5th HOLE

"Lost my wallet with $1,500 here on the 5th last week."

"Reward?"

"Offered $50."

"What happened?"

"Some other guy offered $150."

"If you don't stop that humming, you'll drive me right out of my mind."

"More of a putt, I should think."

Two idiots were playing with their clubs—but no balls.

But they kept an honest score. After each hole, they would say, "I got a four," or "I got a five"—and enter it on the scorecard.

Then argument arose. "What about that air stroke on the fairway?" said one, "You missed the ball completely!"

"That was no whiffie," the other answered, "That was my practice swing."

"Practice swing, my foot," countered the first, "I heard you grunt."

"I don't like the way you cheat on your scorecard."

"Don't *know* any other way."

"Caddy, I'd move heaven and earth to break 100."
"Concentrate on heaven, sir. You've already moved
enough earth."

"You must be absolutely the worst caddy in the whole world."

"I doubt that, sir."

"Why?"

"Too much coincidence."

On the short 5th at Massachusetts' Brae Burn Country Club, a golfer complained bitterly, "My sonofabitch partner cheats!"

"How do you know?"

"He just hit out of the rough with a 3-wood."

"So?"

"I really stepped hard on that ball!"

Then there was the golfer so dumb she looked for diamonds in the rough.

As a twosome moved toward a deep trap on the 5th at the Meon Valley Golf and Country Club in Hampshire, a visiting American heard one of them cautioning, "Easy, Bert. Slow down. Don't let yourself get upset, Bert. Relax."

The American could not resist saying to the speaker, "It's so thoughtful of you to try to keep your partner— Bert—so calm."

"My partner's Alfie. *I'm* Bert."

Then there was the caddy who found he could make more money by lying than by carrying.

On Scotland's windy Carnoustie Course, an American named Stefanovich drove magnificently off the 5th tee. His brand-new ball sailed over the bracken at the dog-leg and out of sight onto the far fairway.

But when he got to where he thought his ball would be—no ball. Just a native golfer who looked suspicious.

"See a ball here?" the American inquired pointedly.

"Nae."

"That ball in your hand?"

"Aye. *My* ball."

"*My* ball had 'Stefanovich' on it."

"A bonnie coincidence, laddie. That's just wha' *I'm* playing this mornin': a 'Stefanovich.'"

"Like my game?"

"I've seen better swings on condemned playgrounds."

"Caddy, why do you keep looking at your watch?"
"Not my watch, sir! My compass."

On the 5th green at Baltray's Country Louth course, Pat turned to Mike. "Shay," he asked, "Which of these two ballsh do I hit?"

"Have anither drink, first, Now how many balls d'y'see?"

"Three!"

"Saints be praised! Hit th' one in th' middle!"

Then there was the nudist golfer who watched TV during the Masters with nothing on.

"Isn't your partner out of that bunker yet? How many strokes did he have?"

"Sixteen. The last one apoplectic."

Then there was the golfer about to putt out on the 5th at Italy's Cervinia Course, who tested the wind, tossed a few blades of grass up in the air, wet his finger, held it up—turned to the caddy and said:

"Dammi il mio pullover, per piaceria."*

* "I'll have my sweater, please."

6th HOLE

Two Americans in Switzerland were playing at 5,700 feet on the Engadine Golf Course. In the thin air, one just couldn't connect with the ball. He'd miss, pick up the ball in his hand and fire it down the fairway. Then he'd walk after it, swing again, miss, pick it up, and throw it on again.

After six holes of this, he finally tossed down his golf bag in disgust and stalked away.

"Hey! C'mon back," called his partner, "You've got a no-hitter going!"

"Like my game?" a golfer queried a fellow player on the 6th at Baltimore's Five Farms Course, "Lessons have cost me $2,500 so far."

"You should get to know my brother-in-law."

"Good golfer?"

"No. Good lawyer."

"Why are you chasing your caddy?"

"We had words. I told him he was a lousy caddy, and he told me, 'You can kiss my ass at high noon.' "

"What's your rush? You still got ten minutes."

Then there was the absent-minded dentist who waited to putt until the cup opened wider.

An American visitor was playing Scotland's Royal Dornoch Golf Club. From the very first tee, he succeeded in sclaffing his ball into every bunker, pond and clump of gorse within range.

On the 6th, he turned to the caddy. "This is the toughest course I've ever played."

"How dae ye ken?" came the reply, "Ye hae na played on it yit."

"Why'd you run into the woods when I cried 'Fore!'?"
"I thought you said, 'Ford!' "

Then there was the very rich Texas golfer who carried fifteen clubs.

On the 6th at the Belle Isle Course near Lynchburg, Va., a golfer found his ball wedged firmly between the roots of a large pine tree.

"Son," he asked his caddy, "What kind of shot do you think this situation calls for?"

"I think I know, sir," replied the caddy, reaching into his bag for the bourbon.

"Reverend, I can't help but marvel at the way you restrain yourself from swearing on the golf course."

"Yes, but where I *spit,* the grass never grows again."

"How long can you go without drinking?"
"About six holes."

"Shaaay, buddy. Where th' hell am I?"
"On the 6th tee."
"Shkip the detailsh. What *coursh*?"

An American tourist playing the short 6th hole on the
Caesarea Golf Course in Israel saw a ball sail past his
head onto the green, rolling within inches of the cup.

He couldn't resist—he tapped it into the hole. Just
then an Israeli golfer came puffing around the corner of
the ancient Roman aqueduct. The American called out,

„ידידי, אתה עומד לחזות בחוית חייך.
בא לכאן ותסתכל בגביע זה.". *

The Israeli came, looked, and yelled down the fairway:

„ברק! השקיע זאת בשבע!". **

* "Friend, you're about to enjoy the thrill of your life! Come over
here, and look in that cup!"

** "Irving! Sank it in *seven*!"

7th HOLE

Pausing on the magnificent 7th hole of the Turnberry Hotel's Arran Course, a Scot was diverted from the breathtaking view of the Strathclyde Coast by screams from a nearby bunker. Rushing over, he discovered a visiting American pinned beneath an overturned golf cart.

"Quick! Get a doctor!" implored the injured man.

"Hae inny insurance man passed by ye yet?"

"No! For God's sake, why?"

"Move over!"

A golf ball is too big to put in a gun, too small to aim properly.

"Fresh kid! I'll report you to the caddy master when we get back."

"By that time I'll probably be too old to caddy, sir."

On the 7th tee of Pacific Palisades' Riviera Golf Club, a novice turned to her companion. "I'm growing a bit tired," she announced, "Let's quit as soon as one of us gets a hole-in-one."

"What was your partner's excuse for that wild putt?"

"All of them."

On the 7th green of the Selsdon Park Golf Club near London, a putting American was suddenly beset by a flock of pigeons from the nearby public park.

He thrashed angrily about with his club, crying, "Fug off, will ya'! Fug off!"

A sweet old lady sitting on a park bench near the green roused herself and came to the fence.

"Oh, sir," she called, "No need to speak to the little birdies like *that*. All you need to say is 'Shoo, shoo, little birdies!' They'll fug off."

A twosome moved aside with some distaste on the 7th green of Carlsbad's La Costa Course to allow a flashily dressed drunk to play through.

To their amazement, the drunk coolly dropped a magnificent 40-foot character builder. Unable to contain themselves, the pair rushed over to offer their congratulations.

"Nothing to it," said the drunk, waving them aside, "With all these holsh out here, how could I miss?"

Then there was the sweet young golfer who drove through the window of a retirement home, and wound up an old maid.

"Every year my game gets worse and worse."

"Why not quit for a year?"

"Can't. Already started on my next year's game."

A golfer on Minneapolis' Minikahda Golf Course missed a 2-foot putt on the 7th hole.

"My God," said his smiling opponent, "I haven't heard such cursing since I was born."

"That must have been a day they *really* had something to curse about."

New Invention: A golf ball that cries out when it gets lost. Just like golfers.

On the 7th at Brancaster's Royal West Norfolk Country Club, a golfer turned to his partner and said, "Could you ask if those two lovely ladies resting near the green might allow us to play through?"

"Ordinarily, I'd be delighted. Except one happens to be my wife and the other my mistress."

"I say! It *is* a small world, isn't it!"

"Why do you play golf?"
"I like to aggravate myself."

8th HOLE

"Now that I'm wealthy enough to afford lost balls," complained an older golfer on the 8th at Houston's Champion Course, "I can't hit them far enough to *lose* them."

"Hale Irwin played here last year," the caddy announced to the American golfer as they approached a lagoon shot on the 8th at the Royal Bangkok Golf Club.

"What would *he* have used on this hole?"

"Playing your game, sir—probably an old ball."

Gerald Ford was once teeing off on the 8th at Burning Tree. As he swung, he did something funny with his left thumb, and the drive went slicing off into the trees and out onto a nearby highway.

The ball smashed through the windshield of a school bus, blinding the driver. The bus struck a truck filled with chickens. Covered with flames, both vehicles tumbled into a deep ravine.

The first State Policeman on the scene ran up to Ford. "My God, Mr. President!" he ejaculated, "Quick, tell me what happened!"

"Well," came the careful reply, "I think I did something funny—like *this*—with my left thumb."

"Caddy, I'm not playing my usual game today."
"What's *that* game called, sir?"

A voice came from the impenetrable rough on the 8th of Brazil's Gavea Course near Rio, "Caddy!"
"Si, senhor?"
"Forget the ball! Find *me* first!"

If you can smile when all around you have lost their heads—you must be the caddy.

"This hole's good for a long drive and a putt," a complacent golfer announced to his caddy on the 8th at Vancouver's Coquitlam Course.

Whereupon he ripped up an enormous divot and watched his ball merely roll to the edge of the tee.

"Now for one hell of a putt," the caddy observed.

"Idiot! Your ball hit me in the eye! I'll sue you for five million dollars!"

"I said 'fore.' "

"I'll take it!"

9th HOLE

An American visitor to Kent's Royal Eastbourne Golf Club rented a set of clubs for his wife—and discovered the pro shop had no bags left to carry them in. Leaving her behind in the clubhouse, the American paired up with a single Englishman.

Holing out on the 9th, he looked across the green to see his wife with another woman on the 3rd. "Aha," he said, "My wife. She seems to have picked up an old bag somewhere."

"Mine, too," replied his partner.

A lone golfer approached the foursome near the 9th green at Los Angeles Bel-Air Country Club and asked, "Mind if I play through?"

"What's your rush?"

"I think my cart battery's running down."

Facing the water at the 9th hole of the Sao Paulo Golf Club, a member of an American foursome called for his 6-iron, and teed up a brand-new ball.

"Corre uma briza forte," said the caddy, "Experimente um ferro numero quatro."*

"Don't be silly," replied the golfer, "Give me my 6."

"Bet a dollar you go in the water," said one of his partners.

"You're on."

"Bet $100 you go in the water," said another partner.

"*You're* on."

"Bet $500 you go in the water," said the last foursome member.

"*You're* on, too. Oh, caddy! Better give me an old ball."

* "Stiff breeze blowing. Try a 4."

On Glamorgan's Royal Porthcawl course in Wales, a man of the cloth blasted out of the 9th hole trap right into another. He pursed his lips quietly.

"Father," said his partner, "That's the most profane silence I ever heard!"

A novice on the links at Italy's Club di Villa Condulmer had never seen a parrot before in his life.

As he drove off the 9th tee, he noticed a bright-plumaged bird sitting atop a nearby olive tree. So he dropped his club, rushed over to the tree, climbed through the branches, removed his cap—and was about to clap it over the parrot, when the bird fixed him with a beady eye, and said, "Che diablo pensi stare facendo?"*

"Mi scuse, signor," the golfer replied hastily, "Ho pensato che lei era un ucello!"**

* "Just what the hell do you think you're doing?"

** "I beg your pardon, sir. I thought you were a bird!"

"I shoot a 72," announced a player filling in a foursome on Fort Lauderdale's municipal golf course.

"Wow!"

But on the first hole, the whizzer actually carded a 6.

On the 9th, picking up his ball in the rough, he called, "So long, guys! Got my 72."

"As your caddy, sir, it's only fair to point out that your play this morning has been strikingly inconsistent."

"Tomorrow's Husband-and-Wife Day. Just getting accustomed."

Before the Back Nine

As you have noticed, there is nothing funny about golf.

Its early history is buried in Obscurity, a rustic village north of Edinburgh. Scots claim the sport originated there in the 15th century, but it actually began indoors as a children's game in Holland. There it was known as *kolf*, or water polo. Other people think it started in the Golf of Mexico.

The Romans played a game like golf—*paganica*. They hit a bag of mashed chicken feathers with a knobkerry and went around in 410. Rome fell the same year.

King James II hated the game. In 1457, he prohibited any Scot from "playeing golfe," that "sik and unprofittable sportis." Also "futeball." Beisbol O.K.

Three Jameses later, word came to Holyrood Castle that French golfing women were going around in less and less—which was certainly the first female golf joke.* So James V shipped the Princess of Scots across the Channel to marry the Dauphin and improve her game.

Mary became a real swinger—soon all the lovesick *cadets* at courts were chasing after her balls. "Cah-day." Get it?

Back at Seton House in Scotland, Mary's second husband, Darnley, missed a critical six-inch putt. Mary strangled him and stuffed him in the cup. She was declared a golf widow and later Elizabeth gave her one stroke.

So much for history.

By 1890, a cloud no bigger than a man's putter was forming over Yonkers, N.Y. The first golf course in the United States—a rude three-holer—was being scraped up (together with other odds and ends) from a cow pasture along the Hudson. Soon, poor people all over the country were asking their friends, "What are golf?"

Their friends replied, "What are Yonkers?"

The U.S.G.A. was founded in 1894 to answer both questions, neither satisfactorily. George Washington was the first president. (You *knew* that.) The Association recommended that the standard golf course be fairly exclusive, 6,000 yards long and separated by eighteen jokes. The object of the game: to drive off the tee (in an

* Hooray for Holyrood!

electric cart) down the fairway towards the green and the pin (*flag*) and cup (*hole*).

When one wishes to strike the golf ball, one dismounts from the cart. Otherwise is polo.

Golf is played by two or four *golfers,* each hitting their own ball. These are *twosomes* and *foursomes*—but if you care about the rules, a twosome is a *single,* while a foursome should use only *one ball* for each pair of partners, alternating strokes. For the past half-century, golf ball manufacturers have been trying to keep that energy-saving fact pretty quiet.

You may well ask, how many golf clubs are there in the United States? About 14. They include the *cleek, jigger, mashie, niblick,* and *baffing spoon.* If you believe that, you'll believe anything. Even funnier things happen on the way to the green—like trees, bushes, ponds, traps, pits and bunkers (Ed. note: *What are bunkers?*). In Africa, *hippopotami* and *rhinoceri.*

Now, play on.

10th HOLE

An American tourist playing with a Buddhist monk on Thailand's Navatanee Golf Course in Bangkok, watched as the cleric bowed before each shot and mumbled a few words.

After a very poor performance on the first nine, the American stared over the rice fields, turned to his partner, and asked, "Holy Father, would it help *me* to pray a little, too?"

"No, my son."

"Why not?"

"Because you're such a lousy putter."

"I suspect our caddy is a thief."

"Wouldn't putt it past him.'"

An American playing Bolivia's Oruro Golf Club—highest in the world—was offered a llama when the Club suddenly ran short of caddies.

"Prepárese," the pro warned him, "A este animal le gusta sentarse sobre las pelotas de golf. Lo que tiene que hacer es meterse debajo de la llama y sacar la pelota. Entonces se levantará y continuará llevando las mazas."*

But during the first nine holes, the golfer had to pull his ball out from under the llama only twice. Then, on the 10th, he drove blind over a hill—and watched the llama gallop out of sight after the ball.

On the other side of the hill, he found the llama sitting up to his neck in a water hazard. Stripping to his shorts, the golfer dove under the llama. No ball. Again and again he dove, gasping for breath. Then he tried pulling on the llama's bridle. The llama just sat there.

Finally the man gave up, swam ashore, and marched to the nearest phone. "What the hell's going on here, anyway?" he yelled at the pro, "I didn't mind going under that llama for my ball now and then, but here I am almost drowned, and the bloody llama's still sitting out in the middle of a water hazard!"

"Oh, señor!" came the reply, "Me olvidé decirle que a él también le gusta sentarse sobre pescado boliviano."**

* "Be prepared. The animal likes to sit on golf balls. But all you have to do is reach under him and remove the ball. Then he'll get up and continue caddying."

** "Oh, sir. I forgot to tell you. He likes to sit on Bolivian fish, too."

"Why is your tongue so green?"
"My partner spilled the Jack Daniels on that last hole."

During a sweltering summer round on Italy's Villa D'Este Golf Course near Lago di Como, a visiting American came upon a fellow player cooling herself rather informally in the 10th hole water hazard.

"Hello, out there," he called, "I believe I've taken you unawares."

"Well," came the angry reply, "you just'a putta' 'em back!"

"You're not really gonna use your putter, sir? It's 250 yards to the green!"

"Wotthehell are you, my caddy—or a surveyor!"

A local about to play the 10th dog-leg at the Killarney Golf and Fishing Club suddenly heard a wee voice at his feet. Looking down, he saw a leprechaun.

"Would ye like to loft your drive over those woods and onto the green for a hole-in-one?" asked the little man.

"I love this game so," the golfer replied, "that I'd give anything in the world for such a favor."

"Then so ye shall, and become Eire's champeen golfer, too! But there is one penalty to pay."

"What's that?"

"Once this gift is given to ye, ye will become impotent."

"Done!" replied the golfer, and sent his drive over the woods and into the cup for an ace.

A year later, having gone on to take all of Eire's prizes, he was again playing the same dog-leg at Killarney, when he once more heard the wee voice at his feet. It was the same leprechaun.

"Ye've become so foine and great," said the little man, "But I must ask. Do you mind at all being impotent?"

"As parish priest at Mulaghareirk, I find it not too much of a hardship."

Then there were the Secret Service men who wanted combat pay for guarding Gerald Ford on the golf course.

"How's my game today, caddy?"

"All I can say, sir: I've seen places on this course I've never seen before."

"Wife says she's leaving if I don't give up golf."

"Whad'ya gonna' do?"

"Miss her like hell."

Playing the 10th hole on Scotland's Prestwick Golf Course in Ayrshire, an American caught up with a local wearing a black armband. "Can I console you?" he asked solicitously.

"Ach, laddie!" came the reply, "Don't tell me ye've found ma' ball!"

"I wish you wouldn't drink so much, sir."
"Whysh that, caddy?"
"I wasn't hired to lug around a bagged golfer."

11th HOLE

A funeral procession wound down the road near the 11th green of the Royal Mid-Surrey Golf Club outside London, just as a twosome member prepared a 30-foot putt.

Without moving an extra muscle, he stroked the ball beautifully into the cup .

"It took iron nerve," his partner congratulated him, "not to let that cortege spoil your shot."

"It wasn't easy," returned the other, "On Saturday, we would have been married twenty-five years."

"What's wrong with my game, caddy?"
"Lifting your elbow too much, sir. On the 19th."

A sailor long marooned on a desert island watched a smashing redhead float ashore on a barrel. "How about a cigarette?" she asked, reaching inside the barrel.

"Wow!"

"And how about a beer?"

"Wow, wow!"

"Now—would you like to play around?"

"Lady, don't tell me you also got golf clubs in that barrel!"

"What are you looking for?" a player asked a drunken golfer.

"My ball."

"But this is the 11th. You weren't playing anywhere near this hole!"

"Lightsh better over here."

"Why are there no worms in any of my divots, caddy?"

"Probably all hiding under the ball, sir."

Two Mexican youngsters watched a golfer blast out of a trap amid the rose bushes on the 11th at Guadalajara.

"Nunca lo logrará," said one.*

But the player did, with a beautifully arcing shot that dropped the ball on the green—and into the cup.

"Oh, muy bien," said the other lad, "Nunca saldrá de ahí."**

* "He won't get out of there."

** "Oh, well. He'll never get out of *that* one."

A foursome on the 11th at Westward Ho!'s Royal North Devon Country Club gallantly suggested to two following American ladies that they play through.

"Why, thanks!" said one, "Go ahead, Sybil, you're up."

"No, my dear. *You* have the honors."

"No, you're wrong. I had an 18."

Then there was the absent-minded English professor who thought that Hemingway's *Across the River and Into the Trees* was a terrible hook.

12th HOLE

Two drunks were negotiating the short 12th at Pine-hurst. One hit a long ball that bounced twice on the fair-way, killed a frog crossing the apron, rolled over the green and dropped past the flag into the cup.

"Got a birdie two on tha' shot," yelled the player.

"Sure did," agreed his partner, "Even knocked the feathers off it!"

"What's your partner doing over that putt, praying?"

"He finished praying long ago. Now he's waiting for an answer."

"How would you play that lie, caddy?"
"Certainly under an assumed name, sir."

"Why d'you think this course is too windy?"
"Would you accept whitecaps in the washers?"

A Japanese golfer blasted out of a sand trap on the 12th at the Takanodai Course to within a foot of the cup.

He putted—and missed!

He broke his club over his knee, threw the ball into the woods, tossed his golf bag into the nearest water hazard, and when he reached the clubhouse, cut his wrists.

Then he grabbed a towel, knotted it around his neck, and hanged himself from a steam pipe behind the lockers.

As the rest of his foursome entered the locker room, one called out:

"Want to play tomollow?"

The suicide quickly reached up and untied the towel. "What time?" he yelled back.

An American named Goldberg, playing alone on France's Chantilly Course, caught up with another golfer on the 8th green. The other saluted him, "Allez-y."

"Goldberg," replied the American, extending his hand. The Frenchman shook it and indicated politely they might play on as a twosome.

At every hole, however, the Frenchman repeated, "Allez-y," to which the American acknowledged, "Goldberg," each time, before proceeding to tee off.

After three holes, it seemed only fair to Goldberg that his new partner should have a turn at the honor. "After you," he said, bowing cordially.

The Frenchman, teeing up, smiled broadly and said, "Goldberg."

A visiting American grew disgusted with his game on the 12th hole of Aberdeenshire's Cruden Bay Golf Club. "Caddy," he cried, "is there anyone in the world worse than me?"

"Aye, sir, there is. But he dinna' nae play."

"I'll need an old ball for this water hole, caddy."

"You haven't had a ball long enough for it to *become* old, sir."

An American golfer, deep in the rough near the 12th green of Africa's Royal Durban Golf Club, heard a loud "thunk" in the underbrush and saw a coconut come sailing out onto the fairway.

Another "thunk," another coconut. And another.

The golfer pushed the bushes aside—and discovered a giant gorilla, smacking coconuts with his baobab shillelagh.

"Eureka!" screamed the golfer, "My fortune's made!"

Three months later the gorilla, properly attired in white shirt, bow tie, knickers and golfing cap, lumbered up to the first tee of the Masters in Atlanta. Snatching his driver from the caddy, he sent the ball screaming 375 yards onto the green, only a few feet from the cup.

The crowd was thunderstruck.

On the green, the gorilla carefully took his putter, bent down, sighted the hole, removed a few blades of grass. Then he straightened up, gently stroked the putter over the ball twice—and smashed it another 375 yards.

"Excuse me," a golfer asked a lovely young thing in a ravine on the 12th at Oakville, Ontario's Glen Abbey Course, "but why don't you help your partner find her ball, so we can play through?"

"She's *found* her ball. Now she's looking for her club."

"Stupid ass, you almost hit my wife!"

"Sorry. Take a shot at mine."

"Nuts!" exclaimed Sigmund Freud when he failed to drop a six-inch putt on the 12th of Austria's Steiermark-ischer Golf Club.

"Siggy!" admonished his partner, "You promised not to talk shop."

13th HOLE

"What the hell does that guy think he's doing, playing off the ladies' tee!" asked a golfer on the 13th at Palm Desert's Eldorado Course.

"It's O.K. He's just back from Denmark. He stopped at nothing to knock off a few strokes."

"Caddy, guess you've gone around with worse golfers than me. Caddy, I said, 'Guess you've gone around with worse golfers than me.'"

"Heard you the first time, sir. Just mulling it over."

"Harry, you've been losing—and finding—that damn ball all day. First in the woods, then under the rocks. Now it's lost somewhere in that swamp. C'mon, give it up!"

"Can't."

"Why not?"

"S'my lucky ball."

"How should I play this putt, caddy?"

"Try to keep it low, sir."

"It's only fair to tell you," announced a golfer to his partner on the 13th hole of Orlando's Bay Hill, "your wife is fickle."

"Now she's thrown *you* over, too?"

A father on "Eire's Eye"—the 13th green of Dublin's Portmanock Course—was counseling his son on temperance in golfing. "D'ye see thim two balls at th' cup? Well, now, if y'were lookin' at thim two, an' saw *four*—ye'd know ye'd taken a drap too much."

"But Da'," replied the boy, "there's only *wan* ball there!"

"First my marriage breaks up. Then I lose my job. But this is the last straw!"

"What's happened?"

"The magic's gone out of my 9-iron."

An American at the Golf Club de Lausanne rejoined his partner, after playing a difficult lie at the bottom of a crevasse on the 13th.

"How many strokes?" asked his opponent.

"Three."

"Three! I heard *six*!"

"Three were echoes."

An American, driving erratically from a grass bunker at Berkhamsted in Hertfordshire, hit and killed a cow in the adjoining pasture.

"My God," he cried, running up, "I'm terrible embarrassed! Can I replace her?"

"Dunno," replied the farmer's boy, "How many gallons a day do *you* give?"

At twilight, a drunken golfer bumped into the lone tree on the edge of the 13th fairway at New Jersey's Atlantic City Golf Course. He backed off—then bumped into the tree again. And again.

"Damnedest course I ever played," he roared, "Right through th' middle of a goddam forest!"

"Do I replace this divot, caddy?"

"Why not just take it home, sir, for putting practice?"

"Shaaay, buddy. Where'sh th' other side of thish golf coursh?"

"Over there."

"S'funny. I was jusht over there. They tol' me it was over *here*."

14th HOLE

A visiting American was playing a difficult approach shot amid the crows on the 14th hole at Manila's Wack-Wack Golf Club. "What club would you suggest?" he asked his Filipino caddy.

"Noong csi Ray Floyd say nandidido noong isang taon, ginoo, nagkaroon din siya ng ganyang suliranin. Ap ginamit ang kanyang anim na bakal."*

So the golfer also used a 6-iron—and fell far short. "I'm short," he muttered angrily at the caddy.

"Opo ginamit din mi ginoong Floyd,"** replied the boy.

* "When Ray Floyd played this course last year, sir, he used a 6-iron on this hole."

** "So was Mr. Floyd."

In the rough near the 14th hole at St. Anne's Royal Lytham Golf Club in Lancashire, two Americans had spent half an hour looking for their lost balls when a little old lady came up and asked, "Would it be cheating if I told you where they are?"

"Who's that older caddy with the beard, dragging the chaise longue along behind us?"
"Caddy, hell. My psychiatrist."

Then there was the golfer so accustomed to shaving his score that he carded his hole-in-one as a zero.

A Scots golfer, driving from the 14th tee on the Queen's Course at Gleneagles, kept duck-hooking his ball into the water hazard.

Unable to correct his swing, and running out of balls, he started borrowing more from his partner. Finally there was nothing left but his partner's package of brand-new balls.

The errant golfer seized one, teed it up—and promptly sliced it into the pond.

"Gie me anither," he commanded.

"Great Scot, Sandy!" his partner replied, "these balls cost me tain shillings apiece!"

"Look, mon. If I've told ye onct, I've told ye a hundret times: If ye canna affaird to play the game, dinna play!"

"Notice any improvement in my game, caddy?"
"Shined your clubs?"

An Englishman playing the 14th on Rhodesia's Bulawayo Course came upon a bed of quicksand from which a native's hand was gesticulating wildly.

"Oh, dear," said the golfer, "I wonder if he's signalling for his wedge?"

"Got a suggestion on my game, caddy?"
"Yessir. Try laying off for thirty days."
"Then what?"
"Then quit."

15th HOLE

An American on the 15th green at Monk's Eleigh Course in Sussex was lining up a putt when a ball whizzed past his ear and into a trap. An Englishman in baggy tweeds came puffing up. "I say," he inquired, "by any chance did you see an errant ball go flying by?"

"Yessiree. But not close enough to read the *name*."

"Sorry, sir. I think we're lost."

"*Lost.* You're supposed to be the best caddy on the course."

"But we've been *off* the course for half an hour."

"Understand you're on the edge of an affair with my wife. Why don't we play the next hole for her?"

"Sure. But let's throw in $100, just to make it interesting."

A visiting American was arguing with his English caddy on Somerset's Burnham and Berrow Course over which club to use on the short 15th—a driver or a 3-iron.

The golfer suddenly seized his driver, swung, and sent the ball screaming into several trees, off a few rocks, and then finally onto the green . . . *and into the cup!*

He turned to the caddy. "See! I *told* you it was the the right club."

Then there was the trigger-happy Mexican pro on the Princess Course at the Club de Golf de Acapulco who got real mad at his partner on the 15th and shot a hole in Juan.

"What shall I do about that bunker, caddy?"
"You should be able to carry it, sir."
"What! All that sand?"

Two Scots lost a ball each on the 3rd water hazard on Macduff's Royal Talair Golf Course in Banffshire. Having no other balls, they decided to continue their play anyway, just by swinging alternately—on the tees, fairways and greens.

All went well until the 15th. They teed off and moved down the fairway. One delivered a mighty swing. An anguished cry went up from his opponent.

"What's tha' matter?"

"Stupid fool. You hit *ma'* ball!"

"Hello, G.B.? Just trying out my new phone on the cart. What hole are you on?"

"The 15th. Hold on a minute; my *other* phone is ringing."

16th HOLE

A millionaire drunk on the 16th at Pennsylvania's Laurel Valley Course came upon two policemen in a hazard, grappling from a rowboat.

"Whaddya' tryin' to find?" he called out.

"A drowned Mafioso, sir."

"Whyda' need one of *them* for?"

A Boston golfer on the 16th at Pebble Beach's Cypress Point Course complained about the heat.

His partner, another Bostonian, chided, "Teddy, remember. We're three thousand miles from the ocean."

An Israeli was lining up a putt on the 16th green at Little Ashton Golf Club in Sutton Coldfield, Warwickshire, when he backed heavily against a British agronomist down on his knees, examining a new strain of bent-grass.

"Please poddon it," said the Israeli.

"Oh my, yes," replied the Briton.

"Mine, too. But please poddon it, anyhoo."

"Want a suggestion regarding your grip?"

"How about around your throat?"

A flying saucer dove steeply into a trap while reconnoitering the 16th hole on Portugal's Quinto do Lago Golf Club in the Algarve. It messaged Mars, "æ#$% £& &£%$#æ?"*

Mars replied, "&£%#æ œ#$% £&!"**

* "How do we get out of this thing?"

** "Try a 9-iron!"

"Some people in Scotland even play golf in the snow."
"Paint their balls black?"
"Nope. Just wear warmer kilts."

Trying to retrieve a lost ball on the 16th at Banff Springs, a wealthy old golfer lost his footing on the edge of a cliff.

Later in the clubhouse, the pro commiserated with the man's nephew. "Were you very close to your uncle?"

"Enough to push."

In the rough on the 16th at Palm Springs' Mission Hills Course, a player was arguing with his partner. "*Two*! I saw you take *six* strokes."

"Four were to kill the rattler."

17th HOLE

On the 17th at the Bahamas Princess Golf Club, a soused player counseled his partner: "After you putt out, don't make my mishtake! Thosh two cartsh at the edge of the green? Get in the right-hand one, or you'll fall flat on your face!"

"Your slice almost hit my head! Why didn't you yell 'fore'?"

"Didn't have time enough."

"You certainly had enough time to yell 'shit'!"

A girl in a wedding gown ran up to a man putting out on the 17th at Cooperstown's Otsego Course, shrieking, "Harry, how could you? Everybody's been waiting at the church for hours!"

"Gladys," said the golfer, "if I told you once, I told you a hundred times—'only if it rains, only if it rains.'"

A brash Hollywood gag writer was teeing up on the 17th—*twice* across the Barry Burn oxbow—at Carnoustie. His distinguished-looking old Scots caddy, who had said little all afternoon, suggested the American use his baffing spoon.

"No *waay*," snapped the jokester, "This yere's a 5-iron shot if I ever seed one," and he smashed away at the ball. It bounced wildly between the Burn, onto the green, and into the cup for a hole-in-one.

"WELLLL!" preened the American, "Whaddya' think of *that* one?"

"It would have been a prettier shot with a baffy, sir," said the old caddy.

"Sonofabitch cheats!"

"How'd'ya know?"

"He lost his ball in the rough and quietly played a new one!"

"You sure?"

"Got his old ball here in my pocket."

Whipped by a gale off the Firth of Forth, a Scot rushed up to a visiting American on the 17th of East Lothian's Muirfield Course, crying: "A bonnie woman's just passed oot on th' next tee. D'ye hae any whisky?"

The golfer quickly produced a small bottle from his bag.

The Scot grabbed it and drained it in a long swallow. "That's a wee bit better. It always make me weakish ta see a woman faint."

Then there was the dramatist on Athens' Glyfada Golf Course who made a play for the caddy.

"What should I do with this divot, caddy?"
"Have you considered growing vegetables?"

"Good Lord! I think your partner's having a stroke."
"Just so he doesn't get it on our card."

On the 17th at the Wentworth Club near Surrey, a foursome member drove repeatedly off the tee into the pond. After his fifth ball went sailing into the water, he threw his driver high in the air, picked up his golf bag, walked to the edge of the hazard, and tossed the bag as far as he could into the water.

His friends stood openmouthed.

The player turned and stalked away.

He had gone about fifty yards toward the clubhouse when he suddenly wheeled, walked back to the edge of the pond, removed his shoes and stockings, rolled up his trousers, and waded out to where his golf bag was still floating on the water. He zipped open one of the side pockets, removed a ring of car keys—and then tossed the bag back into the pond.

"Sorry, old boys," he called, wading out, "I forgot *I* have to drive."

"Shay! We musht be gettin' closher t' th' clubhoush!"
"Hic! How'd ya' know?"
"Cartsh hittin' more golfers."

"Your ball hit me!"
"Not mine, the wife's."
"What're ya' going' to do about it?"
"Want to hit her back?"

18th HOLE

On the Berchtesgaden Golf Course in Germany, a golfer overshot the 18th green. His ball struck a woman sitting on the clubhouse porch. Rushing up to apologize, he discovered he had just killed his wife.

A year later, he played the same course again. As he approached the 18th tee, a fellow golfer recognized him, and remarked sadly, "Heinrich, du willst sicherlich nie vergessen was dir im letzten Jahr an diesem Loch passierte."*

"Du hast recht," came the reply, "Ich habe ein bogey gemacht."**

* "Henry, you'll certainly never forget what happened to you on this hole last year."

** "Damn right. I bogied it."

137

"My friend," said St. Peter to the recently deceased, "you did lead an exemplary life on earth—but there is one instance of your taking the name of The Lord in vain. Would you care to tell us about it?"

"I recall," replied the new applicant, "It was in 1965 on the last hole at Pinehurst. I only needed a par four to break 70 for the first time in my life."

"Was your drive good?" asked St. Peter, with increasing interest.

"Right down the middle. But when I got to my ball, it was plugged deep in a wet rut made by a drunk's golf cart."

"Oh, dear," said St. Peter, "A real sucker! Is that when you . . ."

"No. I'm pretty good with a 3-iron. I played the ball close to my feet, caught the sweet spot and moved it right onto the green. But it bounced on a twig or something—it was a very windy day—and slid off the apron right under the steepest lip of the trap."

"What a pity!" said St. Peter consolingly, "Then *that* must have been when . . ."

"No. I gritted my teeth, dug in with an open stance, swung a smooth outside arc, and backspun a bucket's worth of sand up onto the green. When everything settled down, there was my ball, only ten inches off the cup."

"JESUS CHRIST!" shrieked St. Peter, "Don't tell me *you choked the goddam putt!*"

Then there was the man who married a sweet, innocent thing—only to discover she played a better game of golf than he did. All summer, she bested him. When he shot an 80, she shot a 78. When he shot a 78, she shot a 76.

On Labor Day, she had a ridiculous 40-foot putt to sink, to beat him by one stroke. "Oh, my God," she said, "If I sink this putt, I'll *die*! I'll just *DIE*!"

Her husband looked her right in the eye.

"It's a *gimme*," he said.

Then there was the laundryman who was taken to the cleaners on the 18th.

"Any idea what I should give the caddy?"
"How about your clubs?"

Two friends flew to Hawaii for a week at the Royal Kaanapali Course on Maui. In advance, they agreed that high man would pick up the entire tab for the trip.

On the last day of their vacation, one of the golfers led the other by only two strokes—but still had to sink a 40-foot putt on the 18th hole.

As he started to putt, a mangy-looking Hawaiian dog suddenly trotted out across the sloping green between the ball and the cup. Without blinking, the golfer smoothly completed his stroke—sending his ball in a graceful arc up and around and into the cup by the back door.

His friend could not contain his admiration. "That was the greatest display of coolness under fire I've ever seen on a golf course. You were absolutely magnificent!"

"What coolness?"

"The way you didn't move a muscle when that dog ran out in front of you."

"Good Lord! Was that a REAL dog?"

"What the hell can be done about the traps on this ridiculous course?"

"Start by shutting yours."

A golfer playing the Home Green at Hertfordshire's Moor Park Course turned excitedly to his partner. "I say, old boy, this just has to be a money shot. My mother-in-law's a championship golfer, and there she is on the Mansion steps!"

"A good 400 yards away. You'll never make it."

"What should I give the caddy after we finish the round?"

"How about your clubs?"

"Joe just shot himself?"

"Six strokes up on the 17th! The only way he could lose was if someone turned the course around."

"Wha' happened!"

"Someone turned the course around."

An American was playing a grudge game with an old and boastful Swedish friend at the Östersun-Frösö Golf-klubb. At the 18th, he needed a double eagle to take the game.

Teeing up, he prayed silently, "Please, Lord, let me have this hole, to keep our national pride, and show this loudmouth that Americans are still the best golfers in the world!"

WHAM! He swung from his socks—into which his heart promptly dropped as he watched his drive arc in a mighty slice far off course, bang against a huge rock—and then come sailing back through the air right onto the green.

"Nice going, Lord," he murmured, "Now *I'll* take over."

"Here's a wee something for ye, for a glass of hot whisky," said the Scot as he slipped his caddy a lump of sugar.

19th HOLE

In the dim-lit lounge at the Toledo Inverness Golf Club, a golfer noticed an extremely attractive woman sitting alone at the end of the bar. Emboldened by his third martini, he moved up several stools and asked, "Say, cutie, can I buy you a drink?"

"O.K.," she replied, "But you'll be wasting your time. I'm a lesbian."

"That doesn't bother *me*. How are things in Beirut these days?"

"How do I get someone at this Club to talk to me?"
"Try picking up the wrong ball."

A drunk, almost beet-red in a locker room shower, called to the clubhouse attendant, "Wotthehell's the matter with yer goddam non-lathering soap!"

"Our soap, sir?"

"Been scrubbin for fi'teen minutes, with the hot water on full, and I still can't get any lather outa' this goddam soap!" He held out his hand.

The attendant took a closer look. "But that's not a cake of soap, sir, that's a golf ball."

"A golf ball!" The drunk squinted. "Sonofabitch! But at least you'd think I'd get a *LITTLE* lather out of it!"

"Sorry about this flat on the cart, greenkeeper."
"How'd it happen?"
"Some fool on the 12th had a bottle under his jacket."

"Is my husband there, bartender?"
"No, ma'am. Nobody's husband's here."

"Look at that stupid sonofabitch using a 4-iron on the 18th green! Last jerk who did that drove right through this bar windo—*DUCK!*"

"Heard how Simpkins died on the 12th? His wife put arsenic in his coffee Thermos."
"Great Scott! That's pitiless!"
"Not really. She only filled it with half a cup."

The club souse was watching the Masters on TV in the bar. A guest called loudly, "Hey! Turn up the sound!"
"Shhhh!" replied the drunk, "Not while Ballesteros's *putting!*"

A drunk walked over to the player in the clubhouse bar: "Hoor all ya' fren's?"

"Those are my golf clubs."

"How'd ya' get 'em all t'sit together on *one* stool?"

After a long day on the links, the two buddies finally left the clubhouse bar and wandered down a long, dark hallway. At the end, one accidentally opened the laundry chute door—and fell into the basement locker room.

His friend finally discovered where he had gone. "What'r'ya doin' there?" he called down the chute.

"Changin' my clothes. But look out for th' first shtep. 'S'a sonofabitch."

"Last week I started playing around with my secretary."

"Score?"

"Not yet."

"I once used to shoot 36 holes in a day."

"Terrific! What was your handicap."

"My wife."

On a Connecticut course, a local minister completed a round with the pro. The cleric's game was awful and his opponent was unrelenting. Even in the clubhouse, the pro continued to taunt the minister on his poor performance.

The man of the cloth finally had enough. "Let's play again next week, but this time we'll make it a foursome— invite your parents to join us. Who knows, after the game, I may even marry them."

"Understand Barney Oldfield drove around the world in 1913."

"Not bad—considering the distance."

"Your secretary any good?"

"She was down after only two shots on the 13th."

"Not bad! Then?"

"The greenkeeper came by and made us get dressed."

"Harry planted some great grass in the rough on the 17th."

"What's he trying to do, turn this into a pitch-and-pot course?"

"To what do you owe your success?" the reporter inquired.

"Our Personnel Director," replied the newly-appointed 23-year old corporation president. "Two years ago he dropped my IBM card on the floor of his clubhouse locker room and someone accidentally stepped on it."

"Found a new way to add 50 yards to my drive."

"How's that?"

"Start running before I swing."

The club duffer challenged the pro to a round, asking only that he be allowed two *gotchas*.

After the game, the pro sat sourly in the clubhouse nursing a drink.

"What happened?" another member asked.

"That sonofabitch BEAT me!"

"How *could* he? He's the worst we've got!"

"I was teeing off. Suddenly he grabbed my crotch from behind, and yelled, '*gotcha!*' "

"So?"

"Ever try to play 17 holes waitin' for the second *gotcha*?"

"Where'd Harry get the shiner?"

"He told some player she had the best matched set he'd seen in months."

"Hear Wilkins has big trouble with his putts again."

"The new member's wife, possibly?"

"Her doctor lied. He said if she'd only play without a caddy, she'd develop a figure like Raquel Welch."

"What happened?"

"She developed a figure like Raquel Welch's golf bag."

"Hear the terrible thing that happened to Wilson?"

"Whazzat?"

"Absolutely stunning round Thursday, finished early, showered, drove home—found his wife in bed with another man! Shot them both! Terrible! Terrible!"

"Could have been worse."

"What do you mean, 'Could have been worse'?"

"If he'd finished early on *Wednesday*, he would've shot me!"

An American twosome on Lucerne's Deitchiberg Golf Club finished their round to report to the pro that some other golfer had fallen into a crevasse on the 3rd hole.

"Mein Gott! Iss he all right?"

"Must be. He stopped yelling as we played through."

"Dropped my bottle of Chivas out of the cart somewhere on the 9th, greenkeeper. Was anything turned into lost-and-found?"

"Only the golfer who played after you, sir."

"Last spring I had an overlapping grip problem."

"So why didn't you stay in bed?"

At the Grand Bahama Hotel and Country Club, a visiting American pro fell behind at the casino—and decided to make up his losses on the golf course, hustling an innocent guest.

"How well do you play?" his prey inquired.

"Oh," smiled the pro disarmingly, "Just a hacker. Go in around in 100. Sometimes 98, or 95."

Three hours later he struggled back to the locker room. "That miserable lying sonofabitch," he complained to the attendant, "I had to shoot an 84 to beat him!"

"First the good news. My hole-in-one on the 12th."
"What could be bad after that?"
"151 for the rest of the course."

"I think my future son-in-law is going to be an ass-kisser."
"Whyso?"
"When I drove into a trap on the 11th, with 185 feet to the green over a water hazard—he conceded the putt."

"You've been watching me play for a year. How can I cut about four to six strokes off my score?"
"Leave out one hole."

An argumentative drunk in the clubhouse bar on Houston's Champions Course at Cypress Creek finally threw a punch at a fellow golfer. The other ducked and the drunk fell to the floor. When he'd picked himself up, his opponent had disappeared.

"Not much of a fighter, that guy," the drunk complained.

"Not much of a driver, either," said the bartender, looking out the window, "He just ran his cart over your clubs."

"Did the Tournament Committee approve your score-card."

"No. Just asked for the fiction rights."

"My golf buddy just ran off with my wife."
"You'll find someone else."
"Not someone I can beat so regularly."

"Was Reginald drunk in the locker room?"
"Only trying to get his knickers off over his head."

An American with an enormous bandage under his golf cap sat nursing a double Scotch in the clubhouse bar at Kent's Royal Cinque Ports Course near Deal.

"What happened to you?" asked another golfer.

"You won't believe it. I shanked a slice off the 12th tee into that cow pasture—looked everywhere for my ball—and couldn't find a thing."

"Then?"

"The rather distinguished female playing behind me teed off—but off the pipe, too, right into the pasture. Exactly the same direction my ball took. I thought—if I can only find her ball, I can find mine."

"Yes?"

"Just then, a cow in front of me swished up its tail—*and there was a stuck golf ball!* But it was too far away to be sure it was *mine*."

"So?"

"At that moment, the lady took the pasture fence in a single leap, and asked, 'Have you seen a golf ball?" I walked over, lifted up the cow's tail, and replied, 'Does this look like yours?' My friend, *that's* what happened to me!"

"Tough course?"

"Bet your ass! Even lost four balls in the washers."

"I'm still proud of that drive I hit on the 16th!"

"It's a pity you can't stuff it."

"I gotta bring back that conciliation gift I bought for my wife. Some idiot at the pro shop had engraved it, 'NEVER UP, NEVER IN.' "

"What's wrong with that?"

"That's what she was complaining about in the first place."

"First time on the course? How'd you do?"

"Not bad. Shot a 68."

"Pretty good! Playing tomorrow?"

"Yep. Tomorrow I'm going after the second hole."

"Ach, laddie, I lost ma' bran' new ball today."
"Turrible, turrible, Fergus! Your string broke?"

"Who's s'bes' golfer at th' Club?"
"Harry drunk."
"Second bes'?"
"Harry sober."

"That's our latest member. She's 46-22-32."
"A strange handicap. What's her game?"
"Crawling out on the first tee and trying to stand up."

"He's the world's lousiest golfer."

"Really?"

"Even his tee shots are unplayable lies."

"How come you don't play with Harry any more?"

"How would *you* like to play with a cheat who's always chiseling on his scorecard—and moving the ball with his foot when nobody's looking?"

"Unh, unh!"

"Well, Harry feels the same way."

"For a bunch of golfers, I never saw such huge hands, thick wrists and fat thighs."

"The men aren't much better-looking, either."

"How'd you do today?"

"Terrible. Carded a 12 on the 10th, a 14 on the 11th, a 20 on the 12th—and on the 13th, I blew up completely."

"As a new member, how do you like the greens?"

"Wonderful people!"

"Why's your wife suing for divorce?"

"Some idiot told her I made a five-footer on the practice green."

After the Game

"Phone's ringing, sweetie. Can you roll over and grab it?"

"Sure, George. Probably my husband. *Hello?*"

"Hi, hon. So lovely out here at the Club, I'm staying a few more hours to play an extra round."

"That's fine, darling. Who're you playing with?"

"Oh? My friend George."

"Doc! The baby just got into my golf bag and swallowed all my tees!"

"I'll be right over."

"What should I do meanwhile!"

"Practice putting."

"Home late again. Sorry, dear."

"You and your 'golf buddy' Harry both give me a swift pain. What's the excuse, this time?"

"Nothing but delays, delays—all day. Harry's car had a flat on the way to the course. An enormous line waiting to tee off. The thunderstorm. The hailstorm. The smog alert. Harry dropping dead on the 12th green . . ."

"Harry dropped dead!"

"Yup. And after that, it was just hit the ball . . . drag Harry . . . hit the ball . . . drag Harry—"

Men play golf to escape from (   ) life; (   ) wife; (   ) both.

There's nothing like a game of golf to quiet your nerves, build your muscles, increase your stamina and strengthen your resolve . . . just in case you ever decide to play again.

"Harry, our son says he caddied for you all afternoon."
"Funny. Knew I'd seen that damn kid before."

A visiting American playing Morocco's Royal Dar es Salaam Course suddenly developed the world's worst toothache. Rushing to a local Rabat DDS, he was surprised to find the dentist wanted to fill not only the offending tooth but five or six others.

"Hold on!" he cried, "I'd like to check your work first."

"My pleasure," said the dentist, "Use my phone. Try calling a Mr. Allan Wilson in Secaucus, New Jersey. Three years ago, while he was here on vacation, I filled six of *his* teeth."

After two hours, the phone connection was established and the situation explained to Wilson.

"Weeeeelll," he replied from overseas, "Only yesterday I was playing golf myself. Some clown on the 12th shanked a quail-high ball that came 50 yards and hit me right in the nuts!"

"I'm dreadfully sorry. But—what has *that* got to do with Moroccan dental work?"

"It was the first time in the past three years I forgot how much my teeth hurt."

Then there was the rich Texan who hired a full-time caddy for his electric putting machine.

"Darling, the pro said he liked my equipment."
"What else did he say?"
"Well, that my clubs weren't bad, either."

The sunstruck golfer recovered consciousness while the hospital nurse was reading his temperature: "101 . . . 102 . . . 103 . . . 104 . . ."
"My God," he interrupted, "What's par on this course?"

"This time Harry's probably left me for good."
"But Gladys, he's 'left you' five times already!"
"This time he took his clubs."

"Win at golf today, dear?"

"Well, at least I got to hit the ball more than anyone else."

"Harry plays musical golf."

"Whaddya' mean, musical golf?"

"Goes out on the course fit as a fiddle; comes home tight as a drum."

"What do you think of Jefferson Davis?" the membership committee asked the two new applicants at the Richmond Country Club.

"I really liked the way he blasted out of a trap on the 6th last week," the wife bluffed—and saw her husband shudder.

"Did I say something wrong?" she asked him later.

"You sure did! There is *no* trap on the 6th!"

A retired Oklahoma high roller whose name ended in a vowel was refused membership in an exclusive Phoenix golf club we can call "Riverview." A kindly-disposed committee member suggested the name of an alternate club.

A friend told him, "They probably thought you were Italian."

The oil man, appalled, applied to the second club and was accepted. "And there's one thing I want everybody to know," he announced to the membership committee, "I ain't Italian."

"Whaddya' mean?" said the chairman, "We're *all* Italians here!"

"Well, I'm a sonofabitch!"

"If you'd only mentioned that earlier, you probably could've gotten into Riverview."

"Doc says I'm a physical wreck."

"What did he prescribe?"

"Take time off from golf. Go into the office once in a while."

"Any last request?" asked the hangman of the golfer who had murdered his partner.

"Practice swing?"

An avid golfer flew down to a posh Nassau hotel advertising free golf, free clubs, low room rates.

The rates were low, the food superb, the blackjack dealer forgetful—and the golfing marvelous. In a full week of play on a tough course, he lost only two golf balls supplied by the hotel.

At check-out time, he could not help but ask how the hotel expected to remain in business. Then, as he inspected his bill, his face paled.

"What's this?" he choked, " *Two lost golf balls, $750 apiece, $1500!* "

"At the other hotels," replied the clerk, "they get you by the food; the rates; the blackjack; the green fee. Here . . ."

"Dad, where's the Pebble Beach Golf Club?"
"Ask your Mother. She's always putting things away."

"I hear Harry was held up leaving the clubhouse bar last night!"
"Only way to get him home."

"I used to play golf for days on end, until I met my orthopedist."

"What did he do?"

"Straightened me up."

"You actually, finally beat Harry today!"

"What can I tell you? Next Thanksgiving he and I have a date in Macy's window."

During the Boxing Day Tournament at London's Royal Blackheath Golf Course, an American visitor got into a discussion of scores with a local.

"I haven't broken h'eighty yet," said the Englishman.

"This year?" inquired the American.

"This 'ere wot?"

"Sometimes I get over 900 holes out of a single golf ball."

"I only get about 32."

"Considering your game, not bad."

"Why so sad?"

"Doctor says I can't play golf."

"He's played with you, too?"

"Purist bastards on the Board fined me $200 for striking my wife during the Tournament."

" 'Poor sportmanship'?"

"Nope. Wrong club."

Once there was a man who could never talk about anything but *golf, golf, golf.*

His wife stood it as long as she could. Then one day, she said, "Harry, I'm telling you something for your own good. You are BORING! All you ever talk about is *golf, golf, golf!* Tonight some new friends are coming to dinner. Talk about anything you want. The weather. Politics. You may even talk about sex! But don't, please *don't* talk about golf!"

And at dinner, everyone talked merrily for hours—except Harry, who sat there tight-lipped, staring straight ahead.

Finally, his wife took pity. "Harry," she said, "you look as if you have something on your mind. Like you have something to tell us. What would you like to say, Harry?"

"Do you think," Harry exploded, "Jack Nicklaus made out tonight?"

"Here's a hole for *you*," said the minister as he buried his golf buddy.

Something funny about a game where the player who gets to hit the ball the most always loses.

"That sonofabitch wouldn't even concede a six-inch putt."

"So?"

"Cost me a stroke."

Then there was the exhausted golfer who thought he was only following doctor's orders when he took his iron six times a day.

Sign in a Siamese pro shop: ALSO TEE FOR TWO.

"My game's really improving, dear."
"How's that, Gladys?"
"Today I hit a ball in one."

In the emergency room of the hospital near Scotland's Gullane Golf Course, the doctors were removing a golf ball accidentally driven down the throat of a greenkeeper.

The nurse noticed a golfer pacing outside anxiously. "You're a relative?" she asked.

"Nae. My ball."

"Harry's teaching me how to play golf."

"Smug sonofabitch."

"Right. I felt like killing him today."

"Why didn't you?"

"Didn't know which club to use."

"At your age, I wouldn't think a thing of playing 72 holes a day."

"At my age I don't think too much of it, either."

"Darling, why are you bringing your clubs to *bed*!"

"You *told* me I had to choose."

"Golf's a dumb game!"

"Damn right! Sure glad I don't have to play again until tomorrow."

Bibliography

Anderson, Forrest and Micoleau, Tylere. *Basketball Techniques Illustrated* (New York, 1952).

Bee, Clair, Ed. *Winning Basketball Plays by America's Foremost Coaches* (New York, 1950).

Hobson, Howard A. *Scientific Basketball*, 2nd ed. (New York, 1955).

Holman, Nathan. *Holman on Basketball* (New York, 1950).

National Collegiate Athletic Association. *The Official Basketball Guide* (New York, annually).

Rupp, Adolph A. *Championship Basketball* (New York, 1948).

Weyand, A. M. *The Cavalcade of Basketball* (New York, 1960).

Index

179